BIOGRAPHY of

GEORGE WILLIAM WARVELLE, 1852-1940

I0463525

By Daniel Warvelle Harbaugh, Grandson of George William Warvelle

Biography - George William Warvelle

ISBN 978-1-300-88891-8

90000

Biography - George William Warvelle

FOREWORD

This biography of George William Warvelle was created from documents and photographs meticulously collected and saved over the decades by his daughter and my mother, Marjorie Warvelle Harbaugh. George William Warvelle was truly a great man; a poet, a philosopher, a musician, a thespian, a lawyer, a legal scholar and author of many legal volumes still in print and still found in modern law libraries.

This book encompasses the already excellent biography of George William Warvelle written by Marjorie Warvelle Harbaugh, plus other relevant documents by her and others. The book includes newspaper articles and other printed material of interest; all accomplished via the modern computer era; an era my mother would have mastered and thrived in. Thanks to Microsoft Word, my 'authoring' is more appropriately described as 'assembling components', with my occasional comments added. The book itself follows no particular chronological order; topics, characters and events are presented to fit the occasion.

Biography - George William Warvelle

The WARVELLE family lineage includes **Brissot de Warville**, 1754-1793, a French nobleman and author. After the American Revolution, he visited America and, in 1788, wrote 'New Travels in the United States Of America', an interesting documentary still available in print. During these travels he met and befriended George Washington and Ben Franklin. Returning to France, Brissot was caught up in the French Revolution and beheaded on the guillotine.

Brissot was the family name and Warville the area in France where he was born. He married Felicite Dupont, 1759-1818, of the famous Dupont family. She translated English works into French, including Oliver Goldsmith. They lived in London and had three children.

Brissot was one of the writers who have exerted the most influence on the success of the French Revolution. His early works on legislation, his many pamphlets, speeches in the Legislative Assembly and the Convention, demonstrated dedication to the principles of the French Revolution. His writings included philosophy of law topics and showed the deep influence of ethical precepts.

George William Warvelle had this genetic connection for his philosophy on life. An excellent book 'Brissot de Warville' by Eloise Ellery is still in print.

THE WARVELLE FAMILY PEDIGREE

Jacques Peter Brissott de Warville – Felicite Dupont

Peter Warvelle – Elizabeth Wale

William Wale Warvelle – Eliza Gorry

George William Warvelle

Biography - George William Warvelle

Great Grandfather **William Wale Warvelle**, 1813-1898, and Great Grandmother **Eliza Gorry Warvelle**, 1820-1911, were parents of George William Warvelle.

Great Grandfather **John S. Bangs**, 1812-1861, and Great Grandmother **Margaret Handley Bangs, 1819-1896,** were parents of Lydia Bangs Warvelle, 1853-1925.

Both William Wales Warvelle and John Bangs were craftsman and builders.

First Dane in Racine Built Bangs Bridge

John S. Bangs, who came to Racine in 1839, was the first of a line of scouts who heralded the coming "invasion" of the city by the Danes. Although there were a few Danish men and women here in the forties, and a few more in the fifties, it was not until 1862, and later, that they began to arrive in such numbers as to warrant the use of the above term in connection with their coming. Denmark has sent more of her sons and daughters to swell the population of Racine than any other country: Germany is her only near rival.

John S. Bangs was born in Copenhagen, Denmark, in 1812. He lived in Racine from 1839 to 1857, when he lost his home and other property in the panic of that year, and moved to Holland, Michigan, where he died. While in Racine he was a carpenter and dock builder and contractor, and was one of the substantial citizens of the town. In 1851 he was elected alderman from the Fifth ward. He

Grandmother **Lydia Bangs Warvelle,** 1853-1925, was from a prominent Danish family in Dane County, Wisconsin.

Lydia and George Warvelle with daughters Florence and Effie, 1890.

BIOGRAPHY OF GEORGE WILLIAM WARVELLE

By Marjorie Warvelle Harbaugh, Daughter

George William Warvelle was born May 3, 1852 in Kenosha, Wisconsin, son of William Wale Warvelle, and Eliza Gorry Warvelle. William Wale Warvelle was born in Romney, Kent, England in 1813 and came to America in 1847. His parents were of Anglo-French extraction. Eliza Gorry was born in Port Arlington, Kildare County, Ireland in 1820 and came to America in 1847. Her parents were of Irish extraction.

George William was the oldest of four children: the others following were, Emma, Mary, and Francis Gurry. George Willliam was named after his father's brother, George Peter, and his father, William Wale. He was baptized at St. Mathew's Episcopal Church in Kenosha, of which his father was a very devoted member and his mother a recent convert.

Shortly after his birth his parents came to Chicago and lived on Chicago Avenue in the vicinity of Halsted Street. His father was a carpenter and moved his family to Chicago in the hope there would be greater opportunities for business there than in the little town of Kenosha, or Southport as it was more commonly known. They lived in Chicago only a short while and then retuned once more to Kenosha.

George William at this time was still wearing pinafore gowns. He recalled his grandmother Elizabeth Warvelle as very kind to her little grandson and calling him very brave after a bee sting. A picture of George at the age of eight, his first portrait, shows him to be a handsome, blue eyed, brown curly haired child with a clear rugged completion. In build he is already stocky with a high forehead. His hands were well formed and artistic. His childhood portrait indicated the man he would become.

His parent's home was located on the south side of Kenosha on the shore of Lake Michigan. The house was first a frame house, later replaced by a sturdy brick two story structure opposite Kemper Hall, a girl's boarding school under the Episcopal Church. The homestead consisted of several acres of land and a fine garden. This particular section of the city became the best residential section, and the land very valuable after the Warvelle family property was sold. The yellow brick house is still intact, although it has been moved to another city lot and remodeled by its present owner.

George started to school when he was six, although his mother had already taught him to read and write. Amelia Doolittle was his favorite teacher, and George was under her direction for three years in intermediate and grammar school. Only three of the pupils passed for high school and he was the only boy. Miss Doolittle was advanced to high school and was his favorite teacher again.

Biography - George William Warvelle

Because of an argument and misunderstanding with the school principal, George left school, when was sixteen.

As a child he showed his artistic and studious nature. He drew a picture on the black board of the bombardment of Fort Sumter. The teacher would not let it be erased, for she considered it excellent. The Civil War was still in progress, so the picture was timely and vivid. A young patriot, George wanted to be a drummer boy, but he was too young. As he grew older he became more of a student, reader, and artist. His mother said he was more often seen with a book than without one. His father was most anxious for his son's education and a letter written by him to one of the teachers follows:

August 21, 186

Dear Miss Madora Durkee,
With pleasure I take the opportunity of returning thanks for the interest you have shown in instructing my son George William in this vacation. It always gives us great pleasure that there are those who give of their leisure hours for the instruction of youth, and the good of humanity. I can say with truth that George is a good and willing boy. With respect I give my heartfelt thanks.

William Warvelle

George remembered his early school days most vividly. He hated arithmetic and was a poor scholar in it.

Biography - George William Warvelle

He liked geography immensely and recalled how he would go from St. Petersburg, Russia to Odessa, Russia by water, noting all the capes and headlands. He drilled on the chief rivers and capitols of the world, and never forgot them.. The importance of his daughter's education and the modern system of education appalled him.

He was a good speller, and in the old days of spelling bees, he was one of the ones who remained standing after the battles of words and letters. In fact the spelling of words interested him so that he became a lifelong student of the derivations of English words, and did much research on the subject. Though none of this research has been published, traces of his word studies are evident in his legal and Masonic writings. He was always a profound student of Latin.

He found so many of our common English words come from German and Teutonic origins that he determined to read and write German; this he did after age fifty. He mastered the language in short time, becoming an enthusiastic student of German, and building a large German library of books he had read. His study of the language was accomplished as a hobby in his leisure hours in the evening or holidays. His daughter Effie studied German in high school and university and brushed up on her vocabulary to become a pleasant partner for German conversation and repartee.

Biography - George William Warvelle

Mother listened in and recalled the words she had heard spoken in her community when she lived in Holland Michigan, where the Dutch dialect was spoken. Father enlisted all his German speaking friends and availed himself of every opportunity to express himself in German.

By high school George showed a talent for acting and debating, and joined the Kenosha Literary Society made up of young people who acted out Shakespearian plays. They met at Martin's Library, and performed in Kemper Hall, the town's largest auditorium. George appeared as RICHARD III. He had a deep, rich speaking voice and promising singing voice. He belonged to a choral society, as did his sister and brother, and they enjoyed concerts together in school and church.

While George never had any formal instruction on the piano, he gathered much from his sisters who took piano lessons. He had a fine ear for music and understood music notation and the elements of harmony.

Some of the songs popular in his youth were: 'St Patrick's Day in the Morning', 'Lily Dale', ' Come Cheerful Companion', 'The Minstrel Boy to War Has Gone', ' Belle Malone', 'Neath the Bright Silvery Light of the Moon', and 'Hush My Baby'. All his life he played and sang these simple ballads and folk songs.

Biography - George William Warvelle

Among his favorites in later years were 'The Harp that once through Tara's Halls', 'Then You'll Remember Me', 'Old Dog Tray', 'My Kentucky Morn', 'Old Ned', 'Massa in the Cold, Cold Ground', 'Annie Laurie', 'Kathleen Mavouneen', 'Come Back to Erin', and a host of others including German songs. He especially liked lullabies and composed one he named 'The Virgin's Lullaby, Ave Maria'.

At age 18, after he left high school, he had his first job as a clerk in the dry goods story of Mr. E. C. Brown, and remained there about a year. When he was 19 in 1871, he went to Chicago and acted with a professional company, 'Shakespearean Players' at Mc Vickers Theatre He lived in a room at Wells and Monroe Streets with the rest of the troupe, all young, ambitious and poor.

In October 1871, the Great Chicago Fire occurred; Chicago had a population of about 250,000. George packed his trunk and found a wheelbarrow behind the theatre. He spent the night with the other refugees on the beach at Lake Michigan; now the site of Grant Park. The vividness of the blaze always remained in his memory,. His theatrical career was interrupted by this great fire.

He returned to Kenosha and happened to run into an old friend, George Baxter, a lawyer.

Baxter told George it was time for him to settle down to more serious work than acting.

Baxter offered him a chance to study law in the office of Head and Quarles, both prominent lawyers. Quarles later became a US Senator. George was very fortunate in his choice of teachers as he 'read the law' in the offices of Head and Quarles; he became a lawyer and was admitted to the Wisconsin Bar.

During this period he indulged in some of his artistic tendencies. He and his brother, Gurry, opened a small book store and picture gallery in the business section of Kenosha. The pictures included George's excellent engravings of masterpieces, paintings and etchings. The business lasted briefly until the entire store was destroyed by fire and a total loss. George decided then he wasn't meant to be a business man.

He still liked beautiful pictures, and collected a large portfolio. Some were Victorian subjects, but many were copies of the masters such as Murillo, Gainsborough, Michelangelo and others. Later these pictures found a place on the walls of his home.

Years before he had his home in Chicago, he spent much study on types of furniture and architecture. He kept a scrapbook on interior design and decoration with the popular styles for every room.

Some years later his daughter Marjorie compiled a scrapbook of modern interior decoration and he gave her his book; a treasure, for modern designers as a complete study of the Victorian era and all its beauties and atrocities.

Besides his interests in stage and the fine arts, George showed his versatility and his literary ability in those formative years studying law in the office of Head and Quarles. He became the Editor for the local Kenosha newspaper at the salary of $6.00 a week. He also went on a six week acting tour twice a year to earn money.

While on one of these acting tours he met a young woman who convinced him to enter the abstract office of her fiancé, Mr. Cox. The Haddock, Cox, and Co. Abstract Office was located in Chicago on the corner of Wells and Washington Streets. George served there for three years, and gained the foundation for his later specialty in the law of real property.

During this period that he was asked by the choir master of Our Lady of Sorrows Catholic Church on West Jackson Boulevard to sing in the church choir. This George did, for he was glad to have the fine teaching and experience the choristers were given. He enjoyed learning the Latin psalms, hymns and Gregorian chants.

His training there was a beginning for his lifelong sympathetic understanding and appreciation for the Roman Catholic Church.

From early youth he was a continuous student of the Bible and church history. At one time George considered studying for the Episcopal priesthood, but it was his mother's wish that he study law. Throughout the years he researched the history and prophetic aspects of the Bible and other great bibles of the world and their backgrounds. This pursuit has resulted in his building an extensive biblical library. A large part of his theological studies were applied to Masonic history and practices.

So intense was his research into the philosophies of the Golden Age of the Hellenistic and Roman dynasties and his appreciation of their competing missions and platforms for living, that a group of his close friends and associates pressed him to compile a 'Saints of the World' book; not to dispute the accepted doctrines of Christianity, but to examine the philosophies of the world. The Saints as titled by the church were a subject of continual research by George from their Biblical and legendary sources. His goal was to remove their cloak and veil of sacred tradition to show them in their humanness; especially the Twelve Apostles, the Master and Mother Mary. The later Saints have also claimed his sympathy and consideration; St. Francis of Assisi, Patron Saint of Animals, was his best beloved.

George never indulged in hunting or approved of any sport that made any creature suffer. He shared his companionship with his dogs and hoped to see these old friends in the Hereafter.

In 1875, George returned to Wisconsin and started his law practice in Kenosha, a town of about 5,000 population. In 1877, George married Lydia Ann Bangs in Kenosha. A portrait of the bride shows a young woman of twenty four with dark brown eyes, dark brown wavy hair and olive complexion. She is almost a gypsy type of beauty, quite unusual for her English-Danish ancestry. George and Lydia had known each other from childhood, attended school together, belonged to the same church and literary clubs, and cherished the same teachers, schoolmates, and friends. George's courtship of Lydia was as proper as his legal behavior; neighbors observed he always left her house at 9:00 in the evening.

Their love's young dream had a fitting stage and scene; a re-creation of Oberon and Titania in MIDSUMMER'S NIGHT DREAM, in a neighbor's garden; there George and Lydia plighted their troth.

Lydia's house was that of her Aunt Lydia and her Uncle Abraham Hansen. A portion of that house became George and Lydia's home and they lived there for eight years. Three of their children were born there:, Effie Bangs, Florence Octavia, and Georgia Williamette.

Biography - George William Warvelle

In the memories of this family this home was a haven of cheerful rooms, old fashioned flowers, and kindly neighborhood souls.

In 1873 George and his brother Gurry formed a partnership as 'G.W and F.G.Warvelle, Real Estate Brokers and Financial Agents'. This was dissolved in 1881 when George moved to Chicago and Gurry to the University of Illinois to study. In 1881 George sold his paper, the KENOSHA ADVOCATE for $1000, a princely sum in that era. He left his family in Kenosha and moved his law practice to Chicago where he could have a wider field for his practice. He was admitted to the bar in 1881. The money he had acquired from his sale of the newspaper helped him through that first year in Chicago, where he earned only a few dollars from his legal fees.

He spent his weekends with his family in Kenosha. In the next few years his law practice and income grew and Lydia began taking the children to visit him in Chicago and wondering how they would like to live there. In 1887, the third daughter, little golden-haired and brown eyed Georgia, died of the flu at scarcely three years old. The family moved to Chicago and purchased a new home; a large 10- room, 3-story ornate Victorian brownstone house at 1743 West Monroe Street, in a fine residential neighborhood. George made the remark that he was the poorest man on the block.

Biography - George William Warvelle

George became a mentor of the Chicago Bar Association and American Bar Association. In 1904 he ran for Judge of the Municipal Court on the Democratic ticket. He was the choice of the Chicago Bar Association, but withdrew when he realized the corruption of the political game. This was his only venture into politics; a field he could not practice what he preached to his students or wrote in his law books.

The beacon light in his law career was the immediate acceptance by the local profession of his first book, 'A TREATISE ON ABSTRACTS AND DESCIMATION', published in 1883. It was written during the lean years of his practice when he had his ideals, theories, and judicial advice to offer, but few clients upon whom to practice. There was the urgent need for money for his family; so while waiting for his practice to increase, he put his energy and thinking into this first volume, little thinking it would be such a success and lead him far. The volume became referred to as the 'Abstracter's Bible.'

It was published by Callaghan and Company, Chicago, and thereafter through four printings and three revisions from 1893 to 1910. In 1933, George, then 80, was asked to revise it so that the copyright might be retained by the original publisher. The book was one of the publisher's best selling volumes.

Among other writings which also have attained recognition for George W. Warvelle, both in the courtroom and classroom are:

TREATISE ON VENDORS AND PURCHASERS OF REAL PROPERTY, 1890

PRINCIPALS OF AMERICAN LAW OF REAL PROPERTY, 1895

TREATISE ON THE PRINCIPALS AND PRACTICE OF THE ACTION OF EJECTION AND STATUTORY SUBSTITION, 1900

THE TOTAL OF DISPUTED LAND TITLE, 1900

ESSAYS ON LEGAL ETHICS, 1920

He contributed many articles to local publications, and his texts have been revised from time to time. His volumes may be found in a great number of practicing attorneys in every section of the United States and are referred to similarly to the dictionary and encyclopedia for good advice.

In recognition of his legal literary works, George Warvelle was honored with the following degrees: L.L.D. from St. Ignatius of Loyola University, Chicago, L.D.L. from the University of the Southland, and D.C. L. from De Paul University, Chicago , Illinois.

Biography - George William Warvelle

George W. Warvelle's handwriting was meticulous and beautiful; in publishing his legal texts he did not need to have his script typed. His publishers, Gallaghan and Conway, preferred his handwriting to typed copies as easier for the printers to read than type. George was always particular about his script and deplored the lack of good penmanship in his children. His habit of analyzing each word and phrase as he wrote it, and the study of the derivation of words, was always of great interest to him.

Coincident with his legal writings and legal practice, George Warvelle progressed to Professor of Law and Dean of the Chicago Law School from 1885 to 1902. Professor of Real Property Law in the Illinois College of Law (later De Paul University) from 1903 to 1913, and later a Special Lecturer on Legal Ethics in De Paul University College of Law from 1913 to June 1934.

The Illinois College of Law was organized in 1897, and for fifteen years remained an independent existence without university connection. The College was established by well educated and studious lawyers for the purpose of raising the standards of legal education and preparation for the bar. The College maintained the highest standards for its degree and the instruction was by a faculty distinguished in scholarship and ability as teachers of law. In 1912 the Illinois College of Law was affiliated with De Paul University and in 1915 all departments were transferred to the Tower Building on Michigan Avenue and later to the De Paul University building on East Randolph Street.

George Warvelle's life was spent among young people, first as a student among them and then as their teacher. From the very beginning, he exemplified the ideal teacher. His lectures were a source of interest, inspiration and satisfaction to the hundreds of students privileged to hear him. His students praised him as an 'of-the-people' person. Testimonies and gifts of appreciation from those who learned under him were frequent, especially in his later years; they symbolized a rich reward, and he was honored by their graciousness.

George William Warvelle established his good name in the fullness of his three score and ten years. If being able to look back at his life with satisfaction and contemplate the future with hope constitutes the true richness of life, then George William Warvelle lived abundantly.

George was always fond of his law fraternity brothers in Delta Theta Phi and they fond of him. In his younger days he was a familiar figure around the fireplace of the old chapter house and he entertained the senate for hours with his stories and gentle discussion of the law. Delta Theta Phi later honored him by naming their Chapter the 'Warvelle Senate'.

Biography - George William Warvelle

At the convention in 1913, Dr. Warvelle, a member of the Beta chapter of Alpha Kappa Phi at De Paul University, earned a place in the heart of the national fraternity.

His address delivered at that Chicago convention was considered by those present as a great masterpiece and inspiration to the three fraternities then in process of combining. Naming the 'Warvelle Senate' was a deserved tribute to this distinguished lawyer, scholar and teacher.

" His life was gentle, and the elements so mixed in him, that Nature might stand up and say to all the world: This was a Man"   William Shakespeare

In May 1923, George was honored by his fraternity brothers at the celebration of the 21St anniversary of the founding of Delta Theta Phi at De Paul University. In recognition the 'Warvelle Senate' presented him with framed testament of their appreciation as follows:

'The Delta Theta Phi law fraternity to Dr. George William Wavelle on Founders Day 1923. No words which we now utter, Sir, can add to the honor which is already bestowed on you. Rather, Sir, this is an occasion when we can do no more than reaffirm what your own boys by their actions do affirm and express to you, our admiration for your scholarly achievements, our gratitude for your assistance to the fraternity, and our affectionate regard for you.

We of the Warvelle Senate are unanimous in transmitting this to you, in the hopes that you will honor us on future occasions.'

Here is an example where reward is bestowed on a recipient in time before death or old age delayed it. The old adage is true, 'Now is the time, my friend, no longer wait to scatter loving actions and words of cheer to those around whose lives are now so dear, they may not meet you in the coming year, Now is the time, my friend, now is the time.'

Two more children were born to George and Lydia Warvelle; Gerald Bangs in1894, and Marjorie Bangs in 1897. The son had a tragic life and died early. Through an accident in infancy his brain was injured and he was stunted physically and mentally. He lived to be fourteen. That frustrated life was one to which his father never could be reconciled,, and he bore his grief all through the years and tried to overcome it by cherishing the love and kindness of his friends and especially his young law students, who were to him the son he had lost. Gerald died in 1909, and was followed in 1911 by the untimely death of his beautiful titian haired daughter, Florence Octavia, a promising young art student.

Biography - George William Warvelle

Florence had recently graduated from the Chicago Art Institute with honors, and her father was very proud of her.

Two months after Florence's death, George Warvelle's mother died at age 91. Of her he said she was a most kind and blessed mother and her passing was a peaceful fulfillment of the years; but the passing of his young children was an interrupted vision of hopefulness from which both George and Lydia endured the rest of their lives.

November 12, 1940, was a day of great storms in Chicago. Trees blew down, buildings toppled and ships were wrecked on Lake Michigan. By evening it was calm again. In the old Warvelle home on Monroe Street, the fire burned cheerfully in the library marble fireplace, the radio was on a musical program and all was peaceful. At eight o'clock while sitting in his favorite easy chair, George William Warvelle closed his eyes, and was gone. So closed, in peace and dignity, a life with never a moment of idleness.

His funeral, Saturday morning November 17, was simple and fitting, as he would have preferred. He rested before the altar covered with beautiful flowers amid thoughts of his many friends, as his good friend, Rev. David Gibson, conducted Episcopal services.

G. W. WARVELLE, NOTED TEACHER OF LAW, IS DEAD

Dr. George W. Warvelle, noted lecturer and writer on law, and for 57 years professor of legal ethics at De Paul university, died last night in his home at 1743 Monroe street, his residence for more than half a century. He suffered a heart attack as he was sitting in his library.

Dr. Warvelle, who was in his 89th year, was one of the oldest living 33d degree Masons in the United States. He had lived in Chicago for 60 years, coming here from his native city, Kenosha, Wis., where he had read law in the office of United States Senator Joseph Very Quarles. He was admitted to the Wisconsin bar in 1876.

At a banquet in his honor in 1929, it was said of Dr. Warvelle that more prominent judges, attorneys, and students had taken courses from him than from any other teacher living. Textbooks written by Dr. Warvelle are used in schools thruout the country.

He is survived by two daughters, Miss Effie B. Warvelle, 1743 Monroe street, and Mrs. Marjorie Harbaugh, Hudson, O.

CHICAGO TRIBUNE

Biography - George William Warvelle

In December ,1940, the Paper Book, the publication of Delta Theta Phi, law fraternity, issues that number with an article,"Warvelle Senate Mourn s Namesake", and the cover was one of the last photographs of George Warvelle. It was the same picture they had shown in the October 1929 issue when the Warvelle Senate honored its name-bearer, George Warvelle, in presenting him a testimonial in behalf of Delta Theta Phi, so as the years go on his compatriots remember him.

GEORGE W. WARVELLE
". . . he lived abundantly."

DECEMBER   1940

The PAPER BOOK
DELTA THETA PHI

28

Biography - George William Warvelle

Warvelle Senate Mourns Namesake

Death Comes to Fraternity Leader and Teacher

DR. GEORGE W. WARVELLE, Author, Teacher, Lecturer, Lawyer, Sponsor of Warvelle Senate, Delta Theta Phi, De Paul University, Chicago, died at Chicago, Illinois, on November 13, 1940 in his 89th year.

He was born May 3, 1852 at Kenosha, Wisconsin, the son of William Wale and Eliza Gorry Warvelle. Shortly after his birth his parents came to Chicago, where they resided only a short time and then returned to Kenosha. In his early youth he attended both grammar and high school in Kenosha, leaving high school when he was 16 years of age.

During the Civil War he desired to enlist in the Union Army as a drummer boy but was refused because of his immature age. He was extremely fond of reading, and, as his mother once put it, "he was more often seen with a book than without one." During his high school years he joined the Kenosha Literary Society, who acted out Shakespearean plays. He played the part of Richard III.

After he left high school he went to work as a clerk in a dry goods store for about a year and a half until he was 18 years of age. At 19 he went to Chicago and acted with a professional company in Shakespearean drama at McVicker's Theatre. He was in Chicago at the time of the great fire in 1871 and, with hundreds of others, homeless, he spent the night on Lake Michigan front, now Grant Park. His theatrical career being interrupted by the great fire, he returned to Kenosha and was induced by a lawyer friend to study law. He entered the law office of Head and Quarles, both prominent attorneys, Mr. Quarles later becoming United States Senator. While in the office of Head and Quarles he became a local editor for the newspaper The Kenosha Telegraph at a salary of $6.00 per week. During this time he also went on six-week acting tours twice a year to earn additional money. While on one of these tours he made the acquaintance of one Mr. Cox, member of the abstracting firm of Haddock, Cox and Company located in Chicago. Mr. Cox induced him to take a position with this firm,

which he did for a period of approximately three years. It was here that he gained the foundation for his later specialty in law, that of real property.

In 1876 he was admitted to the Wisconsin Bar and began his practice of law in Kenosha, About this time he also became the publisher of a newspaper with one Myron Baker, first called The Democrat and later changed to Kenosha Advocate.

In 1877 he married Lydia Ann Bangs of Kenosha. Five children were born of this marriage, Effie, Florence, Georgia, Gerald and Marjorie, three of these predeceased their father, namely, Florence 1911, Georgia 1887 and Gerald 1909. Mrs Warvelle died in April 1921. Two daughters, Miss Effie Warvelle and Mrs. Dwight Harbaugh, survive him.

In 1878 he formed a partnership with his brother, Gurry Warvelle, known as "G. W. and F. G. Warvelle, Real Estate Brokers and Financial Agents." This firm was dissolved in 1881 and George Warvelle then went to Chicago. He also sold his paper, the Kenosha Advocate. After coming to Chicago he was admitted to the Bar in Illinois the same year. For six years his family continued to live in Kenosha. In 1887 he purchased a home in Chicago at 1743 West Monroe Street, where he continued to live until his death.

In 1891 he became associated with the law firm of Warvelle, Walsh and Madden. In 1894 this firm was dissolved, and he became associated with Delbert Clithero under the firm name of Warvelle and Clithero. This association continued until 1910, when he retired from active practice in order to devote his time to teaching and his masonic offices.

In 1914 he was a candidate on the democratic ticket for judge of the Municipal Court. Highly endorsed by the Chicago Bar Association, he was not, however, successful in the election.

In 1883 he published his first legal work, a book called A Treatise on Abstracts and Examination of Title. The work was revised in 1907 and 1920. This book was extremely popular and was used extensively

Biography - George William Warvelle

by lawyers and frequently quoted by courts of review.

Other legal writings which also were popular and much used by lawyers and courts were the following:

"A Treatise on Vendors and Purchasers of Real Property," 1890.
"Principles of American Law of Real Property," 1896.
"A Treatise on the Principles and Practice of the Action of Ejectment and Statutory Substitutes. The Trial of Disputed Land Titles," 1905.
"Essays on Legal Ethics," 1920.

He also contributed many articles to legal publications. In recognition of his legal literary work he was honored with the following degrees:

LL.D. from St. Ignatius College of Loyola University, Chicago.
LL.D. from the University of the Southland, University of Alabama, 1896.
D.C.L. from De Paul University, Chicago.

He was Professor of Law and the Dean of the Chicago Law School from 1895 to 1902. Professor of the law of real property at Illinois College of Law (later De Paul University College of Law) from 1903 to 1913, and later a special lecturer on legal ethics at De Paul University College of Law from 1913 to June 1934.

In the year 1906 he was made an honorary member of Beta Chapter, Alpha Kappa Phi Law Fraternity, and in 1913, when Alpha Kappa Phi merged with two other law fraternities to form Delta Theta Phi, Beta Chapter evidenced its love and esteem for its distinguished brother by choosing to name the senate in Delta Theta Phi "Warvelle Senate."

George Warvelle's life was spent among young people, first as a student among them, and then as their teacher. From the very beginning of his teaching days he exemplified the ideal teacher.

His lectures were a source of joy and inspiration to the hundreds of students who were privileged to hear them. He possessed the rare faculty of being able to interest and inspire young men. The students loved him because he was so human and seemed to understand the spirit of youth.

Testimonies and gifts of appreciation from those many who labored under him, especially in his later years, have been frequent. To him they symbolized a rich reward, and he was made happy by these acts of graciousness.

He was always fond of his fraternity brothers in Delta Theta Phi and they were fond of him. In his younger days, he was a familiar figure around the fireplace of the old chapter house, and he entertained the senate for hours with his stories and genial discussion of the law.

Delta Theta Phi had been more to him than just an honor. "Warvelle Senate" meant more than a title.

It was at the amalgamation convention in 1913 when Dr. Warvelle, then a member of the Beta Chapter of Alpha Kappa Phi at De Paul University, earned a place in the heart of the national fraternity.

His address, delivered at that Chicago convention, remembered by those present as a great masterpiece, served as an inspiration to the three fraternities who had the great task of consolidation before them.

In May, 1929, he was honored by "his boys" at the celebration of the twenty-fifth anniversary of the founding of Delta Theta Phi at De Paul University. In recognition, "Warvelle Senate" presented him with a framed testimonial of their appreciation.

He was very much interested in masonry. He was a thirty-third degree mason. He wrote many books on masonry and held many high offices in the various orders of which he was a member.

If to have labored honorably and established a good name, to have won the confidence, esteem and affection and an inspiration to thousands of young men and women, and in the fullness of 88 years to be able to look back at the past with satisfaction—if these constitute the true richness of life, then George W. Warvelle lived abundantly.

Biography - George William Warvelle

In the spring of 1941, the Masonic Oriental Consistency of Chicago presented the two daughters of George Warvelle, Effie and Marjorie, each with a leather bound testimonial in behalf of the Consistency. Those acting on the committee were: William L. Sharp, 33rd Degree, Frank C. Roundy, 33rd Degree, Carl A. Miller, 33rd Degree, Paul F. Erich, 32nd Degree. In this beautifully illumed book, brief but fitting statements were made.

Ill. George William Warvelle 33°
BORN MAY 3rd, 1852
DIED NOVEMBER 12th, 1940

The summons which in GOD's own time comes to all, has called the beloved veteran and Dean of Past Commanders-in-Chief. Your Committee submits the following Tribute to the memory of Ill. George William Warvelle, 33°

Born May 3rd, 1852 – Died November 12th, 1940

How simple the statement, Born! Died! and yet what a history was written between the two, not only a history written in books, but one deeply impressed in the hearts of those who were permitted to associate with him, to know him, and to love him.

His devotion to and his love of Masonry were exemplified during all the years of his activity. To all the various tasks assigned to him, he gave the best that was in him; he lived an honorable life and enjoyed the confidence and esteem of all who knew him; he rendered a valued service to Masonry and earned all the honors that were bestowed upon him.

He was a Past Commander-in-Chief of Oriental Consistory, having served in the years 1894, 1895 and 1896. He was a Past Sovereign Prince of Chicago Council Princes of Jerusalem, serving in the years 1886 and 1887.

He was highly educated and had a keen and discerning mind. His sound judgment, sterling character and strict integrity will ever be an inspiration to his Masonic Associates.

We sorrow with the members of his family and extend to them our deep and heartfelt sympathy in their bereavement. We recommend that this Tribute be made a part of our minutes, appropriately engrossed and given to his two daughters as an expression of our sincere admiration and affection for the friend whom we honored and loved.

Biography - George William Warvelle

In 1994, Gary L. Stuart wrote a 7-page article titled 'Ethics For A New Lawyer'. The article commences with:

"It is not proposed to enter into a discussion of the principles of jurisprudence, but the loose and indiscriminate manner in which the term 'Law' is constantly employed, particularly by writers on moral philosophy, would seem to render necessary at least a passing allusion to that term in connection with morals. Geo. W. Warvelle, L.L.D., Essays on Legal Ethics, Rothman & Co., 1908"

Thus, decades after his death, George William Warvelle is still a current fixture in the legal field. His 'Essays on Legal Ethics' was cited in the 1998 'Tobacco Master Settlement Agreement'.

Ethics For New Lawyer

By: Gary L. Stuart

It is not proposed to enter into a discussion of the principles of jurisprudence, but the loose and indiscriminate manner in which the term "Law" is constantly employed, particularly by writers on moral philosophy, would seem to render necessary at least a passing allusion to that term in connection with morals. Geo. W. Warvelle, L.L.D., *Essays in Legal Ethics*; Rothman & Co., 1908.

Biography - George William Warvelle

After George Warvelle's death. his daughter Effie moved to Hudson , Ohio, and purchased four acres of land and a charming gate house next door to her sister Marjorie. The land was part of the James Ellsworth Estate, a large mansion with gate house, barns, pond, woods and trails. James Ellsworth was a wealthy coal baron and his son, Lincoln Ellsworth, was a famous Anarctic explorer. The gate house was a charming English half timbered stucco type with leaded diamond-paned windows; quite Shakespearean in feeling and suited to a person of such taste as Effie Warvelle.

The old Chicago home passed to new owners who converted it into a rooming house, as befell the fate of most houses in that run down neighborhood. The old library was dismantled, lovely bookcases left behind, but the books found a haven in the Harbaugh home and Effie's new home. Usable furniture was reupholstered and used in Effie's new home. Much was given away or left to fate in the weary old house that had been the Warvelle home for fifty years.

Biography - George William Warvelle

Marjorie Warvelle Harbaugh, daughter of George Warvelle, wrote this about her mother for the family history:

Marjorie in 1953

LYDIA BANGS WARVELLE

Grandmother Lydia passed away on April 11, 1925, in Chicago, Illinois, at the age of 71. With her life story we will trace her days backward; I, her last child, knew her only in her latter days. I was a child of her tumultuous and dreary days, I never knew a youthful mother. For the story of her youth we must ask Effie, her first born. Effie's memories were of her when she knew happiness and beauty in living.

I was twenty seven years old when my mother left this world and when I glance back twenty five of those years, I see my mother, a tall, heavy set figure, with a tanned, sallow face. Her dark brown hair did not become gray in her later years. Her eyes were dark brown, sad, and searching. On her face, grief and suffering were apparent even in my childish appraisal of her.

Mother was 44 when I was born, and three years previously had borne her only son, Gerald Bangs. He became the nemesis in the lives of all the family. His life entwined with the lives of his parents and sisters like a tender vine, always needing protection from our sturdier lives. His short life was unexpectedly ended and the vine withered away; the sickly leaves faded quickly, but the dry tendrils have clung all these years in their sheltered refuge.

Gerald Bangs was born September 17, 1894, Chicago, Illinois. He died January 9, 1911. His short history as overlaps his mother's history will be given with hers. Still, a child born and short lived, not as in aborted embryonic souls, is part of a mother's loving heart. My mother shared of such thwarted efforts, but her greatest burden was that of an imbecilic baby. At thirteen months he was toddling about. At two he was dropped accidently down a flight of stairs by his nurse. From then on complications set in. Her greatest wishes for him were thwarted. At six years he learned to walk again. She felt that if pressure could be lifted from his brain, he would be normal again. However, medical specialists felt his chances for recovery would be slight.

From then on complications set in. Gerald lived in a dwarfed world, a happy disposition child, but the crushed hope of his parents. He died at fourteen quite suddenly from pneumonia and brain congestion. May his soul find expression in a happier existence, He died his mother's son; she gave most of her time and energy to him, which were twice the needs of a normal child. The queer and cruel changes of menopause were heightened by the worry for this tragic child. Gradually the warped memories of the warped boy warped her mind along with the misunderstanding of the father.

Biography - George William Warvelle

The years found her chained by mental torture as well as painful physical infirmities. When her burden was snatched away from her, she was unable to adjust her life to other cares. One life had been frustrated by a frustrated life.

Certain lovely memories of my mother remain flowerlike colorful images. She loved flowers more intensely than anyone I have ever met. The little poem about spending one's last penny for hyacinths instead of bread could have been for her. She could never resist a flower. She could get more joy from a potted geranium than anyone can imagine..All her starved passion for beauty would bloom in that single flower. She had little time for outdoor gardening and enjoyed her all year window garden. Her favorite flowers were: Sweet William, Lilies of the valley, Easter lilies, pansies, and roses. Ferns and ivy were her house plants. She had uncanny luck with making Easter lilies bloom a second time, usually in July.

Her artistic nature found expression in many forms. For weeks beginning before Easter each year we began blowing eggs to keep the shell intact. We ate many eggs, and then after the shells were washed and carefully dried, my father would draw funny faces on them. Then mother would bring forth pretty shades of tissue and crepe paper she saved and make the daintiest little dolls with long, flowing dresses and poke bonnets. Easter dolls were an annual tradition and seemed to supplant the Easter hunt in our home although sometimes we had colored eggs.

Mother in her teens had apprenticed at Fiske Millinery Store in Kenosha, and later came to Chicago to the big Fiske concern which produced the ultra and equal of Paris hats in America during the Victorian era.
She really learned the millinery trade and retained her artistic adeptness in that profession.

Until her late years, Mother always made our hats and they were charming ones in the styles acclaimed. None of my sisters ever thought of buying a hat. Mother simply created the style they wished.

In spite of her eccentric application of her medical knowledge, mother was a medical student and pioneer in bacteriology. She was always reading of new medical discoveries, and was interested in the theory of 'germs' as bacteria was called during those pioneering days. In her youth she studied all the sciences that her schooling afforded, including physiology, and comparative anatomy.

She was interested in nursing too, but this was not encouraged as nursing was held to be a degraded and common profession. The courage of Florence Nightingale in the 1854 Crimean War had not had enough time to become an example of nobility in nursing. Mother was an admirer of Florence Nightingale and often mentioned her and the horrors of the Crimean War. She would have liked to be trained as a nurse, although she realized the work was considered menial.

Mother studied both piano and organ as a young girl. She still played simple melodies from those old wide page books, but her fingers were so cramped from rheumatism she could barely play.

The pieces she played were mostly old hymns and ballads of her youth, such as as 'Rock of Ages', 'There were Ninety Nine and Ninety', 'Abide with Me', 'Listen to the Mocking Bird' and 'When You and I Were Young Maggie'.

As a child she belonged to the Methodist Church, and always adhered to the tenants of the church in that she thought it was wicked to play cards, dance, drink liquor, or use rouge. When she married my father she joined the Episcopal Church and remained a devout member all her life. In her last years her only diversion was attending morning prayer at the Church of the Epiphany where she belonged until her death. She always loved the boy's choirs and the excellent pipe organ in this church. Mother, as early as I can remember, was unorthodox in her ideas of 'closed communion' and the 'common cup'; two points of contention in the Episcopal denomination. However she loved the church and wanted to be left alone in her particular devotions. She always tried to keep Lent by attending many services.

Any extra money she had was put in the alms box for the poor, and no beggar ever went away from her door without a coat and a bit of food. In later years the problems of the poor in the neighborhood worried her heavily.

During her last years, mother made braided rugs. Previously she had saved her old clothes and her children's to be makeovers rather than give them away; but happily they were all changed into rag rugs.

Old outfits, children's coats, woolen blankets, and father's trousers were all assimilated into round or oval rugs for every nook and room in the house. One wonders how she was able to hold the heavy awkward things and sew them with heavy cords, and blunt needles. She enjoyed dying her rugs into bright greens, pinks, blues, and browns. After making dozens of rugs, she exhausted the rag supply, her eyesight dimmed and age crumpled her fingers. Her sewing days were over, but for years later we still used and cherished the rugs.

Of mother's youth one must rely on a few treasured bits of information. She was the eldest of the four children born to John Bangs and Margaret Handley Bangs in Racine Wisconsin. She was born September 16, 1853. The other children were Mary, William Zachariah and John. Her father was a bridge builder and a carpenter. When the children were small the family moved to Holland, Michigan, where he continued his trade.

Her mother's sister, Lydia Handley Hansen, wife of a Methodist minister lived in Kenosha. Aunt Lydia had no children so small Lydia went to live with "Auntie" as she was called. Uncle Abram Hanson was in Africa as the United State Consul to Liberia. He died there in service. Auntie was from every description a kind guardian to her little namesake.

Back in Holland, her father was stricken from a accident with a machine, and died shortly thereafter in 1881, leaving his wife and four children in modest circumstances. Mother was a help to Auntie and in turn Auntie helped the financial burden for her sister's family. The two sisters, Lydia and Margaret always were in close touch with each other. One gleans that they were cultured, quiet, refined English women from a family that little is known of. The Atlantic Ocean made visiting rare, but there were frequent letters from England.

As mother grew up she became absorbed with the interests of the little town she called home, Kenosha. Her aunt gave her many privileges and she had a happy schooling. She went to Kemper Hall, a fine Episcopal girls' school just a few blocks from her aunt's home. At intervals mother returned to spend time with her mother in Holland Michigan. When she was twenty three she spent part of the year there, and taught in the Holland public schools, She was issued a third grade teaching certificate in 1876.

As the years passed she saw little of our mother, and Auntie became her guiding star and remained so until her death. I imagine that in my mother's life she was torn between her filial devotion to her own mother, and living in gratitude to her foster mother. As English widows in America they shared their children's means of livelihood. Mother's sister Minnie and brother William visited occasionally in Kenosha so family contacts were not completely severed.

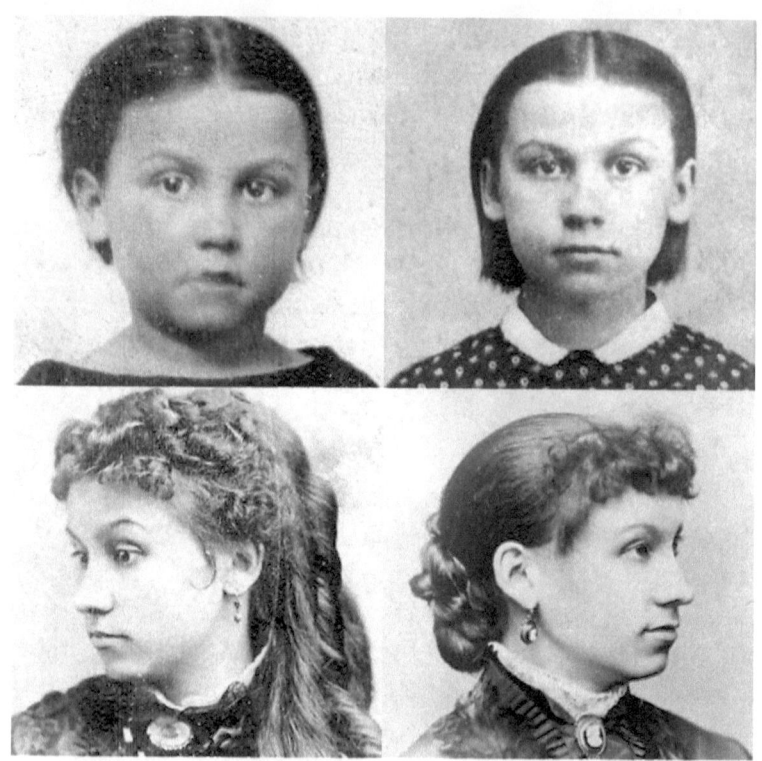

Mrs. George W. Warvelle

Lydia, age 71, a troubled woman, a year before she died in 1925.

De Paul University, College of Law, Chicago. George
Warvelle taught here for 41 years, 1897-1938

Biography - George William Warvelle

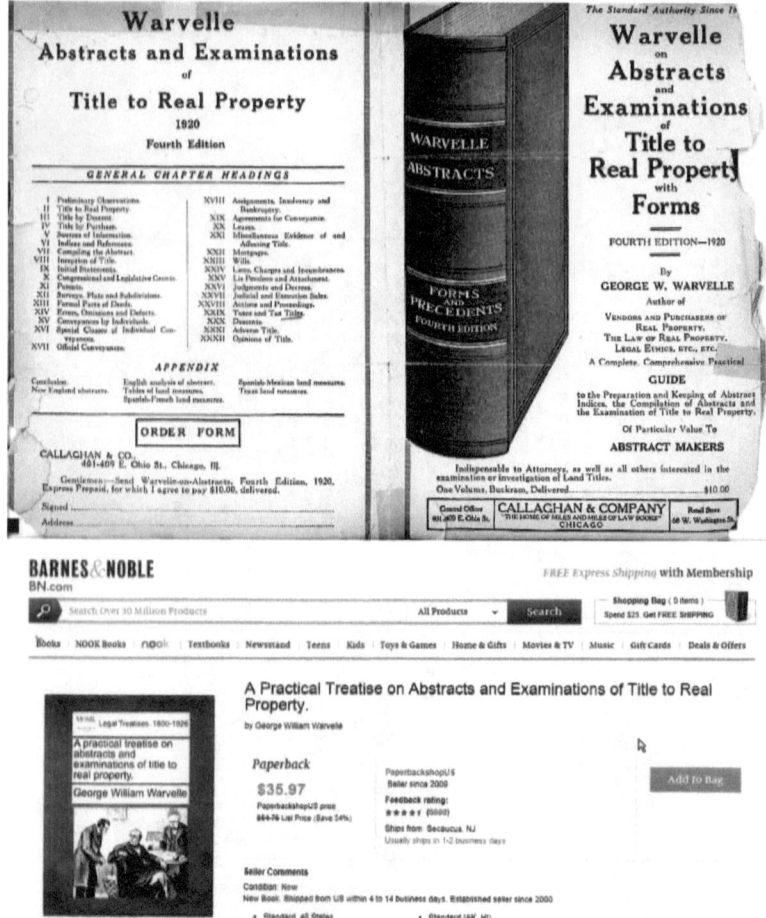

Buy it today at Barnes & Noble. Virtually all of George Warvelle's legal books have been reprinted and are available online; evidence his legal wisdom is still applicable today.

George Warvelle, Shakespearian Actor

Biography - George William Warvelle

George Warvelle and Daniel Warvelle Harbaugh in the Chicago homestead garden, 1929.

The Warvelle Library with ornate white marble fireplace. George Warvelle died peacefully here in his favorite easy chair.

George Warvelle's daughters, Effie, Florence and Marjorie, were accomplished poets. This book, 'Warvelle Reflections', contains 85 of their poems. The book is available online via Google search.

WARVELLE REFLECTIONS

Daniel Warvelle Harbaugh

Biography - George William Warvelle

George Warvelle had two sisters and a brother: Emma Ann, Mary Elizabeth and Francis Gurry Warvelle. Frances Gurry, just called 'Gurry', became a noted geologist and author of geology books.

Science/AAAS | Table of Contents: 29 March 1901; 13 (326) - 2:19pm

PDF »|; THE MINNESOTA ACADEMY OF NATURAL SCIENCES: **F. G. WARVELLE** Science 29 March 1901: 509-510. PDF »|; CHIASMODON IN THE INDIAN OCEAN: H. M. SMITH ...
www.sciencemag.org/content/vol13/issue326/index.dtl - Similar pages - Note this

Science/AAAS | Table of Contents: 28 June 1901; 13 (339)

PDF »|; THE MINNESOTA ACADEMY OF NATURAL SCIENCES: **F. G. WARVELLE** Science 28 June 1901: 1029. PDF »|; GEOLOGY OF CHINA: G. FREDERICK WRIGHT ...
www.sciencemag.org/content/vol13/issue339/index.dtl - Similar pages - Note this
[More results from www.sciencemag.org]

|PDF|

AN ANNOTATED BIBLIOGRAPHY OF POTHOLE FORMS - 2:12pm

File Format: PDF/Adobe Acrobat - View as HTML
of Natural Sciences" by **F.G. Warvelle**,. pp. 509-510. In the northern part of Interestate. Park, there are 70 rock potholes. The ...
sunzi1.lib.hku.hk/hkjo/view/7/700211.pdf - Similar pages - Note this

Mary, 1854-?, married George Rock and little is in the family records about her afterwards.

Emma Ann at about age 16

Biography - George William Warvelle

George Warvelle's sister **Emma Ann Warvelle** married
Peter Nelson and their son **William Warvelle Nelson**
became a noted music bandmaster and popular song
writer. He collaborated on songs with Irving Berlin and
Gus Khan; both famous names in the music business.
His daughter **Warvella Patricia Nelson** resides in
California and visited John Warvelle Harbaugh at
Stanford in 2012. His son **William Warvelle Nelson II**
is a music collaborator with **Willie Nelson**, a popular
singer and performer.

Warvella and father
William Warvelle Nelson

One of many songs by
William Warvelle Nelson

Biography - George William Warvelle

George Warvelle's Great Grand Daughter, Robin Bennett, is of the opinion Gerald Warvelle, George Warvelle's only son, was a classic Down 's syndrome case. The story of the maid dropping Gerald may have been the only plausible explanation in that era.

Robin Bennett , M.S., C.G.C., Ph.D. Hon. Senior **Genetic Counselor** & Co-Director, Genetic Medicine Clinics, University of Washington.

Gerald shortly before his death

Music and sketches by George Warvelle

Biography - George William Warvelle

George Warvelle's last letter to his daughter Marjorie:

QUÆSTORIUM
of the
GRAND IMPERIAL COUNCIL
of the imperial, ecclesiastical and
military orders of the
RED CROSS OF CONSTANTINE
for the United States of America

GEO. W. WARVELLE
GRAND RECORDER
116 N. STATE ST.

CHICAGO, ILL. May 3, 1939

Dear Marjorie

Your kind remembrance and and that of my dear Grand children duly received. I am now the last of the Warvelle family. How soon I must go I cannot say, but as I now enter my 88th year it cannot be very long. But the love of my dear children will last as long as I am permitted to remain. Effie has been very kind to me in my old age and I assure you the she and yourself will always remain dear in my heart. give my love to my dear grand= children.

Your dear Father.

54

POSTSCRIPT

Compiling this biography of my Grandfather George William Warvelle has been to my education and pleasure. Much remains to be discovered in family archives now gradually being found and passed on to me from their guardians over the decades; this book may be revised to accommodate same.

Daniel Warvelle Harbaugh, Houston, Texas 2013

Biography - George William Warvelle

Biography - George William Warvelle

The following Photo Gallery is from an ancient 4-inch x 6-inch photo book compiled by S. W. Truesdell, Photographer, Kenosha, Wisconsin.

George W. Warvelle

Mark Rock

Gurry Warvelle

Mary Rock

Unnamed

Gurry Warvelle

Biography - George William Warvelle

Gurry Warvelle

Emma Warvelle Nelson, Gurry Warvelle, Mary Warvelle Rock

Mary Rock

Unnamed

Mary

Gurry Warvelle

Gorry, Ireland

Biography - George William Warvelle

George W. Warvelle

John Gorry, Ireland

Unnamed

William Wale Warvelle

George W. Warvelle

Mary Warvelle Rock

Emma Warvelle Nelson

Biography - George William Warvelle

Gurry

Emma

Mary, unnamed, Emma

Biography - George William Warvelle

Unnamed

Unnamed

Unnamed

Unnamed

Biography - George William Warvelle

Biography - George William Warvelle

www.ingramcontent.com/pod-product-compliance
Lightning Source LLC
Chambersburg PA
CBHW022124170526
45157CB00004B/1747